NATURE'S CHANGES

25.20/18.80 ea. All 4 for 100.80/75.20
Accelerated Reader Disk:
This is a new series that explains the concepts of change, such as metamorphosis, to young children.
CRABTREE, Grades K-6, 2006, 32 Pages, 8 1/2" x 9 1/2", color photos and illustrations, Table of Contents, Index, and Glossary
SCIENCE & TECHNOLOGY
ANIMAL LIFE CYCLES: GROWING AND CHANGING - Kalman, Bobbie
CHANGING WEATHER: STORMS - MacAulay, Kelley
PLANTS IN DIFFERENT HABITATS - Kalman, Bobbie
WATER CYCLE, THE - Kalman, Bobbie

Nature's Changes

Changing Weather
Storms

Kelley MacAulay & Bobbie Kalman

Crabtree Publishing Company

www.crabtreebooks.com

Created by Bobbie Kalman

Dedicated by Crystal Foxton
To John, Ingrid, Jon, Roberta, Lisa, Albert, Christa, Katrina, and Zach
for your warmth and kindness

Editor-in-Chief
Bobbie Kalman

Writing team
Kelley MacAulay
Bobbie Kalman

Substantive editor
Kathryn Smithyman

Editors
Molly Aloian
Robin Johnson
Rebecca Sjonger

Design
Margaret Amy Salter
Katherine Kantor (front cover)
Samantha Crabtree (back cover)

Production coordinator
Heather Fitzpatrick

Photo research
Crystal Foxton

Consultant
Dr. Richard Cheel, Professor of Earth Sciences, Brock University

Special thanks to
Steve Cruickshanks, Heather Fitzpatrick, David Kanters, and FEMA

Illustrations
Katherine Kantor: pages 11, 12

Photographs
AP/Wide World Photos: page 17
© Holger Wulshlaeger. Image from BigStockPhoto.com: page 30 (top)
Bruce Coleman Inc.: John Hoffman: page 19; Gary Withey: page 22
© CORBIS SYGMA: page 28
© FEMA: page 27 (bottom)
Dave Johnston/Index Stock: page 23 (top)
Bobbie Kalman: page 31
Ted Kinsman/Photo Researchers, Inc.: page 25 (top)
© John Shaw: page 24
Visuals Unlimited: Kenneth Libbrecht: page 13 (snowflakes);
   Gene & Karen Rhoden: pages 14, 20
Other images by Corel, Digital Stock, Digital Vision, Photodisc,
   and Weatherstock

Crabtree Publishing Company

www.crabtreebooks.com   1-800-387-7650

Cataloging-in-Publication Data
MacAulay, Kelley.
   Changing weather: storms / Kelley MacAulay & Bobbie Kalman.
       p. cm. -- (Nature's changes)
   Includes index.
   ISBN-13: 978-0-7787-2280-9 (rlb)
   ISBN-10: 0-7787-2280-5 (rlb)
   ISBN-13: 978-0-7787-2314-1 (pbk)
   ISBN-10: 0-7787-2314-3 (pbk)
   1. Storms--Juvenile literature. I. Kalman, Bobbie. II. Title. III. Series.
QC941.3.M33 2006
551.55--dc22
                                                    2005035794
                                                    LC

**Published in
the United States**
PMB16A
350 Fifth Ave.
Suite 3308
New York, NY
10118

**Published
in Canada**
616 Welland Ave.
St. Catharines, Ontario
Canada
L2M 5V6

**Published in the
United Kingdom**
White Cross Mills
High Town, Lancaster
LA1 4XS
United Kingdom

**Published
in Australia**
386 Mt. Alexander Rd.
Ascot Vale (Melbourne)
VIC 3032

Contents

what is weather?

This girl has prepared for the cold weather by dressing warmly.

What will the weather be like today? Will it be warm or cold? Will it be sunny, or will it be cloudy? Will the wind blow, or will it be calm? Will it rain or snow? We want to know! Many people listen to **weather forecasts** each morning to find out what they should do or how they should dress that day.

Parts of weather

Sunshine, clouds, wind, and **precipitation** are all parts of weather. Precipitation is water that falls from clouds. Rain, snow, and **hail** are types of precipitation. Hail is frozen pellets of ice.

The atmosphere

All weather takes place in the **atmosphere**. The atmosphere is a wide band of air around the Earth. The part of the atmosphere where weather takes place is called the **troposphere** or the **cloud layer**. The troposphere stretches from the surface of the Earth to the area in the sky where clouds form.

troposphere

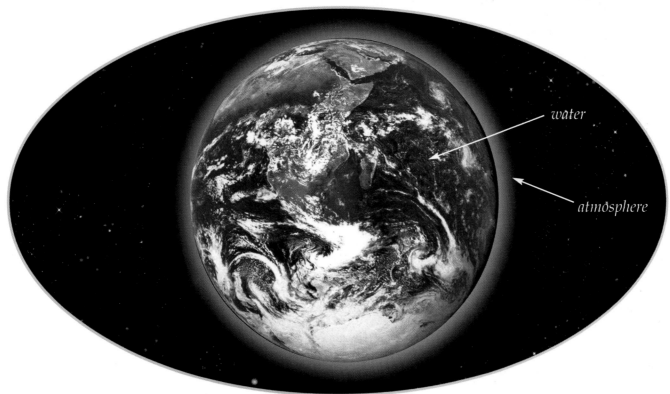

water

atmosphere

Water covers over three-quarters of the Earth's surface! This picture of the Earth was taken from space. The dark blue areas are water. The blue ring around the Earth shows the atmosphere.

The water cycle

Water is an important part of weather. The Sun's heat causes water to change form. When water changes form, the weather often changes, too. There are three forms of water—liquid, solid, and **water vapor**. Rain is liquid water, and snow and ice are solid water. Water vapor is a thin mist of water in the air. The cycle through which water goes as it changes form is called the **water cycle**.

Changing water

Water changes form when the Sun's heat warms the Earth's surface and the air around it. The Sun's heat causes some of the water on Earth to change into water vapor. When wind carries water vapor high into the air, the water vapor gets colder. It changes into clouds. Water falls back to the Earth from the clouds as rain or snow. To see how the water cycle works, look at the picture on the right.

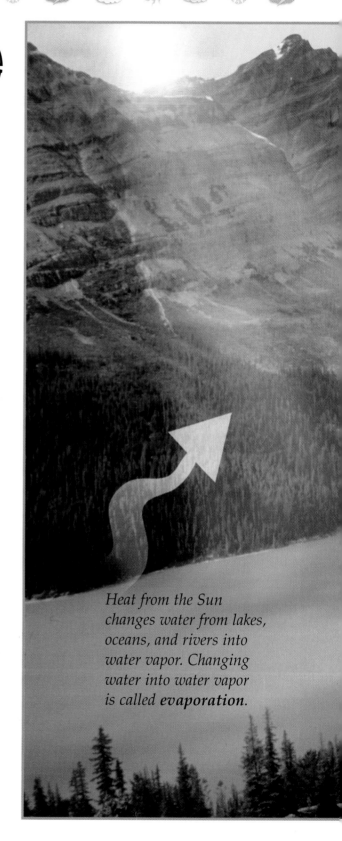

*Heat from the Sun changes water from lakes, oceans, and rivers into water vapor. Changing water into water vapor is called **evaporation**.*

Water vapor in the air forms clouds.

Water from the clouds falls back to Earth as rain or snow.

Water from rain and snow falls into lakes, oceans, and rivers. When the Sun heats this water, it will change into water vapor. With each change, the water cycle continues.

what are storms?

Storms are part of weather. They cause heavy precipitation such as rain, snow, or hail. They also cause strong winds. There are many kinds of storms. These pages show some storms that are common around the world.

Thunderstorms are loud storms! They cause *thunder* and *lightning*.

Tornadoes are fast-swirling columns of wind that stretch from the clouds to the ground.

Blizzards are winter storms with a lot of blowing snow. It is hard to see in a blizzard!

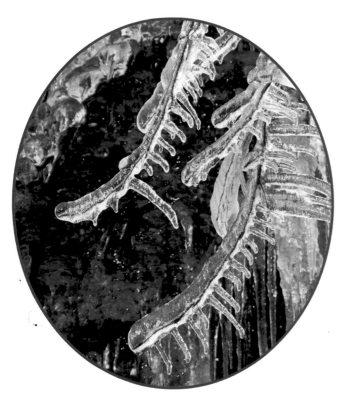

Ice storms leave trees, buildings, and large areas of land covered in thick layers of ice.

Hurricanes form over warm oceans. When they reach land, they cause heavy rain and strong winds.

9

Cloud cover

Before every storm, clouds form in the sky. When the temperature is warm, the clouds are made up of **water droplets**. Water droplets are tiny drops of water. It takes hundreds of water droplets to make a single drop of rain! When the temperature is cold, the clouds are made up mainly of **ice crystals**. Ice crystals are frozen water droplets.

*High in the sky, the temperature is very cold. Clouds that form there are often made up of ice crystals. Clouds made of ice crystals are white and **wispy**, or thin.*

The temperature is usually warmer close to the ground. Clouds that form low in the sky are made up mainly of water droplets. Low clouds are dark gray and cover the whole sky.

How clouds form

Clouds begin to form when the air close to the ground is heated by the Sun and rises into the atmosphere. As the air rises into the sky, it becomes colder. Water droplets form in the cold air. They form around tiny floating things, such as dust, salt from oceans, and **pollen**. The many water droplets that gather together make up the clouds. Look at the diagram on the right to see how clouds form.

2. High in the atmosphere, the air cools. Water droplets form in the air.

3. When many water droplets form, clouds appear in the sky.

1. Air near the earth is heated by the Sun. It rises into the atmosphere.

*Scientists study the shapes and colors of clouds to discover what kinds of storms may take place. Huge, circular storm clouds cause **severe**, or harsh, thunderstorms. A severe thunderstorm is called a **supercell storm**.*

Precipitation

Almost all storms cause some kind of precipitation. Precipitation falls from clouds to the ground. It can reach the ground in solid or liquid form. Sometimes, precipitation is a mixture of liquid and solid water. This kind of precipitation is called **sleet**. These pages show how rain and snow form inside clouds.

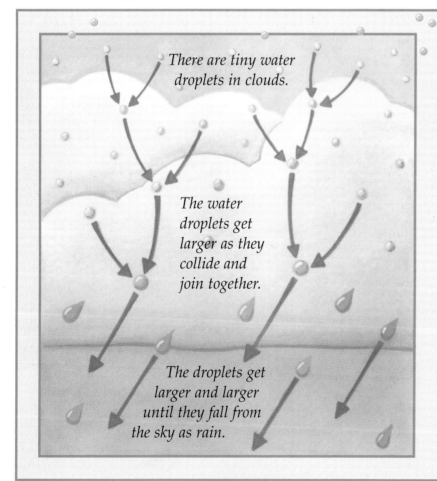

There are tiny water droplets in clouds.

The water droplets get larger as they collide and join together.

The droplets get larger and larger until they fall from the sky as rain.

Forming raindrops

Raindrops are made up of water droplets. Raindrops form when water droplets inside clouds bump into one another. This bumping is called **collision**. During a collision, the water droplets stick together and form larger droplets. After many collisions, the droplets are the size of raindrops. Raindrops are too heavy to stay inside clouds. As a result, they fall to the ground. The diagram on the left shows how water droplets collide to form raindrops.

Forming snowflakes

Snowflakes are made up of ice crystals. Ice crystals are heavier than water droplets are. Soon after ice crystals form, they begin to fall from clouds. As ice crystals fall, they collide and join together. The ice crystals collide many times, getting larger each time. When many falling ice crystals join together, they form a snowflake. Some snowflakes are made up of as many as 200 ice crystals!

Each one of these snowflakes is made up of many ice crystals, and each one is different.

*The ground is almost always covered with snow at the **North Pole** and at the **South Pole**.*

Wild Wind

Wind is a powerful part of a storm. During a storm, the wind blows around snow or rain violently. It can destroy buildings and **uproot** trees. Wind is created by the Sun's heat. When the Sun's rays heat the air, the air begins moving.

The warmed air rises into the atmosphere. As the warm air rises, cold air rushes in underneath the warm air, close to the Earth's surface. This rushing air is wind.

The violent winds of a tornado can easily rip apart homes and farms.

Friction

The Earth's surface is covered with trees, hills, mountains, and buildings. As wind moves over the Earth, it rubs against these surfaces. This rubbing is called **friction**. Friction slows down the wind. In areas where the Earth's surface is flat, the wind blows much faster.

Strong winds rubbing against these rocks have shaped the rocks over many years.

15

Electric skies

Thunderstorms are common during spring and summer. They usually occur in the afternoon or in the evening. Thunderstorms may cause heavy rain, strong winds, lightning, and thunder. Some thunderstorms last for up to two hours, but most last for only fifteen to 30 minutes.

A building storm

Thunderstorms begin with tall, dark clouds. The clouds are created by **updrafts**, or warm, fast-rising air. When heavy rain falls from the storm clouds, it creates **downdrafts**, or air that is quickly moving back down toward the Earth.

Sound and fury

As a thunderstorm's updrafts and downdrafts rush past each other in the clouds, the water droplets and ice crystals in the clouds are moved around violently. These violent motions cause **electricity** to build up in the clouds. When too much electricity builds up, it is released as lightning. Lightning is a giant bolt of electricity. Lightning creates thunder. Thunder is the noise that lightning makes as it travels through air.

When lightning strikes trees, it often splits them in half, as shown above. Once a tree is split, it may fall across a road or onto a house. Trees struck by lightning may also catch fire.

Hailstorms

During **hailstorms**, the ground becomes covered with hail. Most hailstorms take place before thunderstorms. Hailstorms last only about fifteen minutes, but they can cause a lot of damage in a short time! Each year, hailstorms injure people, kill animals, damage cars and buildings, and destroy **crops**.

*Hail is made up of **hailstones**. A hailstone can be as small as a pea or as large as a baseball. This hailstone is over four inches (10 cm) wide!*

The windshield of this car was damaged by large hailstones that fell during a hailstorm.

How does hail form?

Hail forms only in **cumulonimbus clouds**, which are very cold. Hailstones form when raindrops are carried through clouds on updrafts and downdrafts. As raindrops fall through the clouds, they freeze into tiny ice pellets. When the pellets reach the bottom of the clouds, updrafts carry the pellets back to the top of the clouds. Downdrafts then carry the pellets down through the clouds again, and another layer of ice forms on the pellets. The pellets move up and down through the clouds many times. They get larger each time. Eventually, the pellets become chunks of ice that are too heavy for the updrafts to lift. The chunks of ice then fall to the ground as hail.

Hail can fall at speeds of over 100 miles per hour (161 kph)!

Twirling tornadoes

Tornadoes are violent storms that begin as **funnel clouds**. Funnel clouds are columns of fast-spinning air. They drop down from clouds during thunderstorms. When funnel clouds strike the ground, they are called tornadoes. Tornadoes form only during supercell storms. Supercell storms have strong updrafts. The storms cause heavy rain and hail.

Destructive winds

A tornado's strength is measured on a scale that ranges from F-0 to F-5. The scale measures the tornado's wind speed. An F-0 tornado is the weakest kind of tornado. It has winds of 40 to 72 miles per hour (64-116 kph). Winds this strong can break windows and uproot small trees. An F-5 tornado is the strongest kind of tornado. It has winds of 261 to 318 miles per hour (420-512 kph)! These winds can rip apart concrete buildings.

Tornado Alley

Tornado Alley is an area in the United States where most of the tornadoes on Earth take place. It stretches from Texas to Iowa. More than 1,000 tornadoes form in Tornado Alley each year! **Tornado season** lasts from March to August. Tornado season is the time of year during which most tornadoes form. Tornadoes can occur at any time of the year, however.

Most tornadoes last only a few minutes. Even brief tornadoes can cause a lot of damage, however. They violently blow around everything in their paths. Tornadoes easily rip apart buildings, knock over trees, and toss cars through the air. This picture shows damage caused by a tornado.

Freezing blizzards

Blizzards are winter storms that cause heavy snow, cold temperatures, and winds that are stronger than 35 miles per hour (56 kph). These violent winds blow around the falling snow.

They also whip up snow that is already on the ground. The snow blows into deep piles called **snowdrifts**. Snowdrifts can bury cars and cover doorways, causing people to be trapped in their cars or houses.

During blizzards, blowing snow often makes it difficult for drivers to see. It also causes roads to be slippery.

Biting cold

During a blizzard, the freezing winds can make temperatures feel even colder than they are. When a person is out in these winds, his or her body heat is lowered. When a person's body heat is lowered, he or she is at risk of getting **frostbite**. Frostbite is an injury to a person's skin caused by cold temperatures. Frostbite usually occurs on noses, ears, fingers, and toes. The picture on the right shows some toes that have been injured by frostbite.

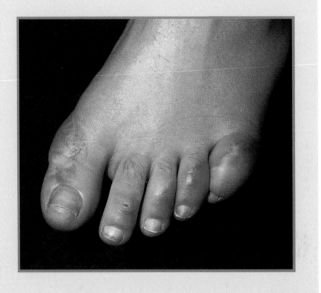

Some animals, such as this bison, have thick layers of fur on their bodies to protect them from a blizzard's cold winds. Deep snowdrifts can make it difficult for animals to move and find food after blizzards.

Covered with ice

Ice storms are winter storms that cover huge areas of land with thick layers of ice. Ice storms are caused by **freezing rain** that falls for at least twelve straight hours. Freezing rain is rain that changes into ice when it hits the ground. Ice storms usually occur between late fall and early spring. An ice storm can cover an area of land that is as large as 30 miles (48 km) wide and 300 miles (483 km) long!

Heavy loads

After an ice storm, the ice on trees, buildings, and roads can cause a lot of damage. The ice is heavy and slippery. It can sometimes be so heavy that it causes trees and the roofs of buildings to collapse. Sidewalks and roads become as slippery as skating rinks, making walking and driving difficult. When the ice freezes electrical wires, **blackouts** can occur.

This tree was covered by ice during an ice storm. The weight of the ice caused the tree to split apart.

glaze ice

Two kinds of ice

Two kinds of ice can form during ice storms— **glaze ice** and **rime ice**. Glaze ice is **transparent**, or see-through. It is thick and solid. Rime ice is white in color. It is not as smooth or solid as glaze ice is. Rime ice is less destructive than glaze ice is because it is easier to remove, and it melts more quickly.

rime ice

Horrible hurricanes

The image above was taken from space. It shows a hurricane moving toward land.

Hurricanes are the most destructive storms on Earth. A hurricane is a large storm with fast-moving winds. It also causes heavy rain and **storm surges** (see page 27). Hurricanes usually last about six days. They form over warm oceans and cause a lot of damage when they **make landfall**, or blow onto land. Hurricanes occur in many parts of the world. They have different names in different places. For example, in eastern Asia, hurricanes are called "cyclones."

Storm surges

A storm surge is a large amount of ocean water that is pushed toward shore by the strong winds of a hurricane. On land, the fast-moving waters cause floods, such as the one shown left.

After a storm surge, flood waters can wash away people's homes.

Hurricanes Katrina and Rita

In 2005, two of the most powerful hurricanes in United States history struck the **Gulf Coast**. On August 29, Hurricane Katrina ripped apart cities in Louisiana, Mississippi, and Alabama. Over a thousand people died, and thousands of survivors were left stranded for days without food or water. The storm surge destroyed the **levees** around New Orleans, Louisiana, leaving most of the city flooded. A few weeks later, Hurricane Rita roared onto the coasts of Florida, Texas, and Louisiana. This hurricane also left thousands of survivors without homes, businesses, or schools.

FEMA workers and U.S. soldiers helped rescue stranded people after New Orleans was flooded by Hurricane Katrina.

studying storms

Scientists who study storms and other kinds of weather are called **meteorologists**. By studying storms, meteorologists can learn about what causes storms and what makes them destructive. If scientists know what causes storms, they can warn people when dangerous storms are forming. Advanced warning gives people time to travel to safe areas.

This scientist is studying a hurricane. He is using an instrument to measure the hurricane's wind speed.

Gathering information

Scientists have many ways of learning about the weather. For example, **Doppler radars**, such as the one shown left, are scattered throughout the world. These radars send out signals in their areas. Some of the signals bounce back to the radars after hitting precipitation, such as rain, snow, or hail, in the air. When the signals return to the radars, they create pictures that are sent to huge computers at weather stations. Scientists at the stations study the pictures, as shown below. The scientists use radio and television to warn people about dangerous weather conditions.

Trouble ahead!

Many scientists believe that **global warming** is changing the weather all over the world. Global warming is the warming of the Earth and its oceans. The actions of people are causing the Earth to heat up. People burn huge amounts of fuels such as coal, oil, and gas to heat their homes, run their cars, and to get electricity. When these fuels are burned, they create **pollution** that traps heat in the Earth's atmosphere. The trapped heat raises the temperatures of the Earth and its oceans.

People cut down forests to make paper, lumber, and to make room for farmland. Cutting down forests makes global warming worse. Trees absorb pollution from the air. Without forests, there are fewer trees to remove pollution from the air.

Severe storms

As the Earth gets warmer, storms are getting bigger. Storms such as hurricanes get their power from warm ocean waters. Warmer oceans produce hurricanes that are more powerful and destructive. The added heat in the atmosphere also creates more supercell storms. These huge storms cause severe thunder and lightning, as well as tornadoes.

Take action!

Anyone can help stop global warming! One of the best ways to help is to **conserve** fuel. To conserve means to use less. You and your family can conserve fuel by walking, riding bicycles, or taking public transit instead of driving cars. Turning off stereos, television sets, computers, and lights are other ways to conserve. Also, remember that you can save trees by not wasting paper!

Bicycling with your family is a good way to help stop global warming, and it is also fun!

Words to Know

Note: Boldfaced words that are defined in the text may not appear on this page.

blackout A loss of electrical power to a community

crops Plants that are grown for food

cumulonimbus clouds Tall, dark, and cold clouds that can cause hailstorms and thunderstorms

electricity One of the basic forms of energy

FEMA The Federal Emergency Management Agency, an organization that helps communities in the United States recover from disasters

Gulf Coast The region of the United States that borders on the Gulf of Mexico

levee A wall built around a city to keep out water

lightning A bolt of electricity that is released from clouds

North Pole An area at the most northern part of Earth

pollen A powdery substance found in flowers

pollution Harmful materials that can make soil, air, and water unclean

South Pole An area at the most southern part of Earth

thunder The sound lightning makes as it travels through air

uproot To knock over a tree, pulling its roots from the ground

weather forecast A report explaining what the weather will be like on a particular day

Index

1 2 3 4 5 6 7 8 9 0   Printed in the U.S.A. 5 4 3 2 1 0 9 8 7 6